THE EXQUISITE ART OF UNNECESSARY SUFFERING

so_to_speak

The Exquisite Art of Unnecessary Suffering

tellwell

Tellwell Talent
www.tellwell.ca

ISBN
978-0-2288-7519-2 (Hardcover)
978-0-2288-7520-8 (Paperback)
978-0-2288-7518-5 (eBook)

THIS ONE'S FOR THE ARTISTS
OF DARKNESS OVERCOME
WE'VE FOUND A HOME
IN ONE ANOTHER
A HOME IN POEMS
MY SOUL IS KNOWN
BECAUSE OF YOU

PART: ZERO

[-A DEDICATION.]

[-OUR MEMOIR.]

SHE OPENED HER WOMB

I TODDLED IN

BUT IT WAS MADE OF ASH

PART: ONE

[-THE EATING OF COALS.]

WHAT A LUXURY
IT MUST BE
TO SAY LIFE IS JUST TOO SHORT
I CARVED TALLY MARKS
INTO THE BEDPOST
BEHIND MY PILLOW
BACK WHEN I WAS EIGHT
COUNTING DOWN THE DAYS
UNTIL SWEET RELEASE

[-MIDNIGHT MOLASSES.]

I HIDE
HER IN THE CATACOMBS
OF MY MIND
UNHOLY ROYALTY
THE TORTUROUS CORPSE
THAT ALWAYS SEEMS
TO FIND ME
NO MATTER HOW MANY
MOUNDS OF DIRT
I LAY ON TOP OF IT
SHE FINDS ME IN
HAND-SHAKES AND
SELF-WORTH QUAKES AND
IN COLD TONGUES
I ASK MY FRAGILE HEART
IF A DAY WILL ARRIVE
WHEN IT KNOWS
IT SURVIVED
HER - WHEN IT KNOWS
IT IS NO LONGER YOUNG
SHE POSSESSES
EVERYONE AROUND ME
THEIR FACES JUST
MAD MASKS
OF HER SUPREMACY
I BREATHE
IN THE POISONED GAS
OF HER MEMORY
OF HER ETERNAL GHOST
EACH VOICE A HOST
OF HER OWN
AND I'M STILL UNGROWN
I'M STILL THAT KID
UNDER THE BED

[-AND SHE'S STILL
ALWAYS HOME.]

SHE /S/L/I/C/E/S/ THE MIND
BUTCHER OF MINE
QUEEN OF SERPENTINE SWINE
RELEASED IN THE NIGHT
SNAKES DRAGGGGGGGGGGGING PIGS BEHIND
SLITHER. SLUMP.
SLITHER SLUMP SLIME.
DEMON EYES ALIGN AND
I DIE ONE BITE AT A TIME
DOWN THEIR LONG NECKS I SLIDE
INTO THEIR GLUTTONOUS
SEDENTARY BELLIES
THEY DIGEST ME
THEN RE-AWAKEN ME
FOR ANOTHER DAY OF TORTURE
RESURRECTED PREY FOR HER
BUTCHER OF MINE
QUEEN OF TURPENTINE TWINE
MY MOUTH WRAPPED UP TIGHT
SHE DARES ME TO SET IT ALIGHT

[-SOMEDAY I MIGHT.]

I WAS ALWAYS
WALKING AROUND
WITH A BED ON MY HEAD
I THOUGHT I WAS CLEVER
BUT SHE COULD
ALWAYS FIND ME WHEREVER
WHEN SHE WANTED TO
I COULDN'T HIDE FROM HER
I TRIED TO TELL ON HER
ONCE BUT
THERE'S NOTHING TO DO
ABOUT INVISIBLE WOUNDS

[-IS THERE?]

I ALWAYS WONDERED WHY

I WAS NEVER AFRAID OF

THE MONSTERS UNDER THE BED

THE WAY THE OTHER KIDS

SEEMED TO BE

DON'T GET ME WRONG

I KNEW THEY WERE THERE

THEY JUST WEREN'T SCARY

NEITHER WERE THE HORRORS
SHE SHOWED ME ON THE TV SCREEN

LIKE

THE GIRL POSSESSED BY SATAN

OR

THE GIRL HAVING SATAN'S BABY

OR

WORST OF ALL THE GIRL WHO GOT HER PERIOD IN THE GYM SHOWER AND DIDN'T KNOW WHAT IT WAS AND ALL THE OTHER GIRLS LAUGHED AT HER AND HER MOM LOCKED HER UP FOR BEING DIRTY

MAYBE

I SAW MYSELF IN THEM I SAW THEM IN ME AND
I THINK I KNEW

THE
        MONSTERS
UNDER
        MY
BED
        WERE
JUST
        TRY-
ING
        TO
HIDE
        FROM
HER
        TOO

[-LITTLE GIRL BLUE.]

I FOUND THEM UNDER THE BED
NEXT TO THE DUST BUNNIES
AND BOXES OF PHOTOGRAPHS
AND UNREQUITED PROMISES
I FOUND US ALL HOSTAGES
THE VERSIONS OF ME
I HAD CREATED TO ESCAPE
I FOUND MY EGO STATES
OR DID THEY FIND ME?

[-
DIS
SO
CI ATED
W E
.]

I WILL CLOSE THEIR EMERALD EYES TO THE FADING CHAOS

TELL THEM EPHEMERAL LIES STIRRED UP ONLY FOR US

BREW UP A NEW CUP OF SOME POTION - SOME TINCTURE

ESCAPE THROUGH THE VAST MAGIC
OF THE GRAND MOTION PICTURE

I WILL TAKE THEM
TO THE LAND OF ENCHANTED ECHOES

I WILL BAIT THEM
WITH THE SAND OF SEASHORES WELL KNOWN

BEWITCH THE RUDE TRUTH WITH OUR OWN DÉJÀ-VOODOO

UNSTITCH THE DOLL THE WITCH
CURSED HER ILL-WILL INTO

A YOUNG HEART GONE CALLOUS - A LOST ALICE

TOSSED DOWN THE WELL OF EVER-AFTER-MADNESS

I'LL BE THE BOSS-BITCH OF MY MADE-UP PALACE

JUST WAIT AND SEE

WE WILL PLAY OUR TELE-STORIES ON LOOP-DE-LOOP

ALL THE DEAD MARIONETTES DO WHAT WE TELL THEM TO

FUCK SICK INFLICTORS AND
THEIR UNPREDICTABLE ATTACKS

WE ARE GREAT PREDICTORS
WITH TRICKSY ELIXIRS FOR SNACKS

WE WILL POSSESS
THEIR FICTIONAL SOULS WITH OUR OWN

RESURRECT INTO FICTIONAL FRIENDS EVER WELL KNOWN

WE WILL NEVER HAVE TO FACE THAT SCARY PAIN AGAIN

JUST HIT REPLAY

REPLAY

REPLAY

REPLAY

RE-

PLAY

[-ARE YOU STILL WATCHING???

OU STILL WATCHING???

ILL WATCHING???]

I KEEP ALL OUR OLD PHOTOGRAPHS
BUT ALL I SEE ARE GHOSTS
IT FEELS AS THOUGH THAT REALM AND THIS ONE
ARE DRIFTING RATHER CLOSE
FUNNY HOW
I STILL SEEM
TO LIVE IN-
SIDE OF BOTH

PART: ONE.FIVE
[-A COGNITION INTERMISSION.]

PAIN PLOWS A PATH
DOWN TO MADNESS
AND MADNESS
IS A GRAVE
A GLASS COFFIN
OF DECAY

PART: TWO
[-THE FILLING OF HOLES.]

THE CHILD GRIMM GLARES
AT THE DILUTED FAIRY TALES
UP ON THE MOTION PICTURE BOX
BEMUSED

THE DISNEY-FIED DREAMS
DON'T SEEM TO CAPTURE ME
THE PURIFIED STREAMS
CAN'T SEEM TO BAPTIZE ME

I WANDER FROM THE FANTASTICAL CASTLE INTO
THE
FOREST
OF
ENCHANTING
PAIN

I DRINK THE NUMBING POTION AND
DIVE
IN
DEEP

IT TASTES LIKE HOME HERE

MESMERIZED
BY THE POISONED VINES
I CLIMB UNFAZED

A MANIACAL MASTER OF THE MAZE I
CLIMB. IN. DEEP.

IT FEELS LIKE HOME HERE

THE THORNS SLICE THE SAME WAY HER WORDS DID
THE SAME WAY HER MEMORY SLICES NOW
BECAUSE THREE'S A CROWD

THE ANIMALS' REPLIES AS SILENT AS MINE WERE
THE SAME WAY I STILL STAY QUIET NOW
BECAUSE SHE'S TOO LOUD

MY TEETH BITE MY LIPS UNTIL THEY BLEED AND IT

SINKS. IN. DEEP.

IT SOUNDS LIKE HOME HERE

I LUST OVER THE LONELINESS
GLUTTONOUS I EAT TOO MUCH
THEN NOT ENOUGH

I TRUST IN THE HOPELESSNESS
INSATIABLE I DRINK TOO MUCH
THEN THROW IT UP

THERE IS NO FIRST-KISS-UNDER-MOONLIGHT HERE
JUST HER BIRTH-CURSE-UNDER-CRUELNIGHT FEAR

CONFESSION FEELS TOO MUCH LIKE A BLANK STATEMENT
DEPRESSION FEELS LIKE TOO COLD OF A BLANKET
BUT THE DARKNESS IS WHATEVER I MAKE OF IT
AN OLD FAMILIAR FRIEND I NEVER WISH TO ESCAPE

[-ENCHANTING PAIN.]

I HAUNT THE ROTTED COTTAGE IN THE FOREST
THEY TRY TO VISIT ME BUT
THERE IS NO CLEAR PATH AMONG A FLOOR OF THORNS
THEY TRY TO SCREAM FOR ME BUT
THERE IS NO CLEAR PATH AMONG A TANGLE OF TREES
THEY GIVE UP ON ME AND
I LIKE BEING GIVEN UP ON
I LIKE WISHING UPON THE MOON
TO TAKE ME SOON
I LIKE BATHING IN THE NIGHT
I LIKE KISSING AWAY THE LIGHT
I LIKE IT WHEN IT'S STARLESS
SOMEDAY THEY'LL FEED UPON MY
HEARTLESS
CARCASS
REGARDLESS

[-DAUGHTER OF DARKNESS.]

LIKE A CHILD TO THE FLAME, I HAVE TO TOUCH IT
YEARNING TO PUT MY HEAD IN THE OVEN
JUST TO BE NOTICED
BUT ALL THE BOYS
CHASE THE SKINNY GIRLS
AT RECESS ANYWAY
AND DISILLUSIONED LITTLE GIRLS
DON'T REALLY KNOW HOW TO PLAY
I RUN CLUMSILY ON TREADMILLS
AT 4TH GRADE POOL PARTIES
CHASING THE START
OF SOME NEW STORY
I LIKE
MOVIE-THEATER POPCORN
WITH LIQUID BUTTER
IT KEEPS MY MOUTH TOO FULL
TO SCREAM OUT FOR MY MOTHER

THE WEIGHT
BECOMES A GREAT
INVISIBILITY CLOAK

IT KEEPS ME ALONE

THERE'S SO MUCH SNOW
INSIDE THIS GLOBE

MY TEARS FREEZE
BEFORE THEY EVER
HIT
THE
GROUND

AND
I
STILL
CAN'T
MAKE
A
SOUND

NOT A PEEP, LITTLE SHEEP

LIKE A CHILD TO THE VASE, I HAVE TO TOUCH IT
BURNING TO BREAK MY OWN HEART
JUST TO BE NOTICED
BUT ALL THE BOYS
CHASE THE ROOFIED GIRLS
IN DARK BARS ANYWAY
AND PRUDE LITTLE GIRLS
DON'T REALLY KNOW THE RULES OF THE GAME
I RUN ON SYNTHETIC DRUGS
AT TOP-GRADE SEX PARTIES
CHASING THE START
OF SOME NEW STORY
I LIKE
LAXATIVES DISSOLVED
IN MY TEQUILA
IT KEEPS MY SOUL TOO EMPTY
FOR ME TO REACH IN AND FEEL IT

THE WEIGHT
BECOMES A GREAT
INVISIBILITY CLOAK

IT KEEPS ME ALONE

THERE'S SO MUCH SNOW
INSIDE THIS GLOBE

MY TEARS FREEZE
BEFORE THEY EVER
HIT
THE
GROUND

AND
I
STILL
CAN'T
MAKE
A
SOUND

NOT A PEEP, LITTLE SHEEP

LIKE A CHILD TO MY SHAME, I HAVE TO TOUCH IT
PICKING SCABBED ARMS & ACNE SCARS
JUST TO BE NOTICED
BUT ALL THE BOYS
CHASE THE PRETTY GIRLS
DOWN TO THE ALTAR ANYWAY
AND DEATH-SET LITTLE GIRLS
DON'T REALLY KNOW HOW TO WAIT
I RUN ON BROKEN HEELS
AWAY FROM MY OWN PARTY
CHASING THE START
OF SOME NEW STORY
I LIKE
SEARCHING FOR BITTER DOUBT
IN THEIR GUARANTEES
IT KEEPS MY LIPS TOO PURSED
FOR THEM TO BE ABLE TO KISS ME

THE WEIGHT
BECOMES A GREAT
INVISIBILITY CLOAK

IT KEEPS ME ALONE

THERE'S SO MUCH SNOW
INSIDE THIS GLOBE

MY TEARS FREEZE
BEFORE THEY EVER
HIT
THE
GROUND

AND
I
STILL
CAN'T
MAKE
A
SOUND

NOT A PEEP, LITTLE SHEEP

SO IF TO LOVE IS TO PAY ATTENTION
I GUESS I'M FUCKED
I WANT IT ALL JUST A LITTLE TOO MUCH
I WANT IT NOT ENOUGH

AND I'M NOT TOO GOOD AT THIS STUFF

I KEEP SCREAMING
BUT IT DOESN'T SEEM LIKE ANYONE CAN HEAR ME
AND MAYBE I GAVE UP
JUST A LITTLE TOO EARLY

MAYBE I GAVE UP
BEFORE I COULD EVER EVEN
BREAK GROUND

[-MAYBE ONCE SNOWGLOBE GIRLS ARE TRAPPED
THEY'RE NEVER FOUND.]

SO I PRESENTED MYSELF ON A PRISTINE PLATTER

THE MONSTERS MUNCHED & MUNCHED
& MOUNTED ME MADDER

THE GOBLINS GOBBLED & GOBBLED
& GRIPPED ME GLADDER

THEY ALL FED ON FUCKING, FEELING FATTER & FATTER

AS I FASTED-FELL-FAMISHED & SUNK SADDER & SADDER

THE CHILD GRIMM BECAME PRINCESS SLIM

AND LIVED MADLY EVER-AFTER

[-LET'S FEAST, BEASTS.]

THEY WANTED TO
EAT ME UP
SWALLOW ME WHOLE
LIKE A MONSTER
FROM A STORY
FOR CHILDREN
THEY WERE STARVING
AND I WAS MADE OF DEAD FLESH
BUT THAT'S NOT LOVE

[-IT'S JUST CANNIBALISM.]

THE RABBIT SHAKES
OFF THE TRAUMA
OF SURVIVING
THE BEAST'S ATTACK

THE HEALING COM-
PLETES ITSELF - COMES
FULL CIRCLE WITH
THIS ONE SACRED ACT

MEANWHILE I TAKE
JUST A SIP (SHOT)
OR TWO OR FIVE
TO CALM MY NERVES

[-BUT I NEVER STOP SHAKING.]

I PRAY TO THE GOD OF OZ
BUT IT'S JUST
GREEN BILE IN THE TOILET
I SOILED IT
WITH MISSHAPEN MISTAKES
OF MIDNIGHT'S PAST
ALAS I CLICK MY
RUBY-RED SLIPPERS
BUT I THINK THEY'RE WHY
I SLIPPED HERE
I'M NOT SURE HOW
THESE FEET GOT
SO SUDDENLY BLOODY
I THROW TOTO A BONE
BUT WE ARE STILL
SO FAR FROM HOME
AND I DON'T
THINK THIS RUN-ON STANZA
WILL GET US BACK TO KANSAS

WAS I LOOKING FOR A BRAIN OR A HEART
OR THE COURAGE NOT TO FALL APART?
I THINK THIS LACK OF SOBRIETY
HAS FINALLY STOLEN MY SANITY
AND I'M NOT SURE
WHAT REALITY IS
ANYMORE

[-SO I'LL JUST STAY HERE ON THIS BATHROOM FLOOR.]

JACKED-UP JILL

                        HILL
                THE
        UP
WENT

TO FETCH AN EVER-AFTER

SHE BROKE HER CROWN

SHE
        FELL
                BACK
                        DOWN

[-AND THE MADNESS
        CAME T U M B L I N G
                AFTER HERRRRR.]

CHILD GRIMM AND LADY SLIM
PLAY WITH
MADAME MAUSOLEUM
AM.I.ME? OR AM.I.THEM?
I'M NOT SURE AGAIN
I'M NOT SURE WHEN
I BECAME HER THEN
SHE BECAME WE'RE
WE'RE NOT HERE WE'RE.TEARS.

WE'RE LOST IN
R I VE RS
OF EVERCLEAR WE'RE TOSSED IN RIVERS
OF EVERFEAR
UNCLEAR WHO'S HER

I CAN'T BE ME I CAN'T BE ME I CAN'T BE ME I
CAN'T BE ME

WE ARE HER WE'RE [-WE'RE.]

TEETER TOTTERRRRRRRR

TOTTER TEEEETER

WHICH ME WILL
COME OUT TO PLAY? WHICH ME WILL
NEVER SHOW HER FACE?????

WE
TEETER TOTTER
TEETER TOTT
ER
BACK AND FORTH
WE
ARE SLAUGHTERSOP ON THIS WATER-
BOARD WE SWISH TOGETHER BACK AND FORTH WE
SWITCH TOGETHER BACK AND FORTH WE
AREN'T SURE WHICH ONE OF US IS ME
ANYMORE

WHO WILL END UP ON TOP?

DOES IT REALLY MATTER.

THAT WOOD WILL TURN
UP STRAIGHT SOON ANYWAY THAT WOOD
WILL TURN INTO A
STAKE SOON ANYWAY

AND THEN WE'LL BOTH BURN

[-BUT FOR NOW WE

JUST KEEP ON

TAK-

ING

TURNSSSSSSSSSSSSSSSSSSS.]

ALL THE PRETTY BALLERINAS LIVE IN LOCKBOXES
I KEEP THEM ALL IN PRETTY CHESTS INSIDE MY CHEST
THEY TELL THEIR LIES TO ME IN PRETTY PARADOXES
AND ALL THE BOYS SAY I'M REAL PRETTY TOO

NO ONE SEEMS TO HEAR THEM
TWIRLING UP IN THERE BUT ME
I KEEP THEM ALL IN PRETTY BEDS INSIDE MY HEAD
THEY SELL THEIR LIES TO ME IN PRETTY INCONGRUITIES
AND ALL THE GIRLS SAY I'M REAL PRETTY TOO

THEY ALL CALL IN HYENIC YELPS OF SWEET DECEPTION
I KEEP THEM ALL IN PRETTY HOLES INSIDE MY SOUL
THEY YELL THEIR LIES TO ME
IN PRETTY CONTRADICTIONS
AND EVERYONE SAYS I'M REAL HYENIC TOO

AND I'M NOT SURE WHICH OF THEIR
VOICES IS MINE IF ANY SO-
I RIP OFF THEIR PRETTY HEADS.I DROWN
THEM ALL TILL THEY'RE DEAD

[-WITH MY BUCKETS OF BORDERLINE-BOMBING BOOZE.]

THE WHEELS ARE A BIT TOO WOBBLY TODAY
    SO ARE THE ONES SPINNING UP
    INSIDE OF MY BRAIN

THERE'S NO WAY TO KEEP
THIS DAMN SHOPPING CART STRAIGHT
    I CAN'T SEEM TO KEEP
    THESE DAMN VOICES STRAIGHT EITHER

AND I'M PRETTY SURE
I'VE BEEN DOWN THIS AISLE
FIVE TIMES ALREADY

I THOUGHT I KNEW WHAT I NEEDED WHEN I CAME HERE
    JUST A BOTTLE OF TEQUILA AND SOME COLD BEER
THEY'RE OUT OF STOCK BUT THAT DOESN'T REALLY MATTER
    I CAN'T SEEM TO KEEP THINGS THAT MATTER EITHER

I GUESS I'LL JUST KEEP
SEARCHING IN OLD PLACES FOR A NEW CURE

[-I THINK I GET THAT FROM HER.]

THEY HAND ME THE BROKEN ROSES FOR FREE
DOWN AT THE SUPERMARKET
AND IT ALWAYS TAKES A MINUTE
FOR ME TO FIGURE OUT
WHAT IS WRONG WITH THEM
AND THEN I SEE IT
IT'S A
HOLE IN A PETAL
OR IT'S A
BEND IN THE STEM
I SEE MYSELF IN THEM
MAYBE THAT'S WHY
I'M ALWAYS TRYING
TO GIVE MYSELF AWAY FOR FREE TOO

[–I THINK I GET THAT FROM HER TOO.]

ORIGAMI BODY FOLDED ODDLY
FLUTTERS (SHUTTERS) IN THE KILL/KILN (DRAGONBREATH)
CAUGHT IN THE LEG
OF THE KITCHEN TABLE
I'VE BEEN HIDING UNDER

STILL AN EIGHT-YEAR-OLD IN A GROWN-UP BODY

I TAKE LESS AND LESS AND
DREAM OF BEING SPACELESS
CLEAN UP THE HEARTMESS AND
GET MYSELF DRESSED

ORIGAMI BODY FOLDED HOTLY
FLUTTERS (SHUTTERS) IN THE JIZZ/MIST (DRAGONSPIT)
CAUGHT IN THE PEG
OF THE WICKED BOY/MAN
I'VE BEEN HIDING UNDER

STILL A SIXTEEN-YEAR-OLD IN A GROWN-UP BODY

I TAKE LESS AND LESS AND
DREAM OF BEING TAKELESS
CLEAN UP THE HEARTMESS AND
GET MYSELF DRESSED

ORIGAMI BODY FOLDED STARVING
FLUTTERS (SHUTTERS) IN THE GIN/BINGE (DRAGONSHIT)
CAUGHT IN THE KEG
OF THE STRICKEN BUZZ/NUMB
I'VE BEEN HIDING UNDER

STILL A TWENTY-TWO-YEAR-OLD IN A GROWN-UP BODY

I TAKE LESS AND LESS AND
DREAM OF BEING WEIGHTLESS
CLEAN UP THE HEARTMESS AND
GET MYSELF DRESSED

I FOLD MYSELF

UPON MYSELF

UPON MYSELF

UPON MYSELF

SOMEDAY
I' LL REALIZE
I DON' T
HAVE TO STAY HERE
I DON' T
HAVE TO WAIT HERE
I' M A
WEIGHT-ER
I' M A
PAPER
AIRPLANE

]

.

E

I WILL
FLY AWAY C
I' LL BE

A

P

S

[-

LET'S HIDE IN THE CAVE
WE CAN CAVE INSIDE OURSELVES
WE CAN BE THE CAVE
I THINK THOSE ARE TEARS
RUNNING DOWN YOUR FACE
I CAN SEE THEM
THROUGH THE WINDOWS OF MY EYES
HERE INSIDE THIS PLACE
TRAPPED IN THIS HEADSPACE
BUT EVEN IF WE ESCAPED
WE'D STILL CRAVE THE CAVE
AND THAT'S OK
SOMETIMES IT'S OK TO HIDE
AND IT'S OK TO CRY

PART: TWO.FIVE
[-A COGNITION INTERMISSION.]

THERE IS A SADNESS
WHICH RISES WITH THE DAWN
ISN'T THERE, LITTLE ONE
THE MADNESS ABANDONS AND
YOU'RE LEFT THERE ALL ALONE

PART: THREE
[-THE PAYING OF TOLLS.]

WITHIN THE WOODS
A CLEARING
A FIELD OF
HONEYSUCKLE & BLOODY KNUCKLES

WHAT DID IT COST TO GET HERE?

THERE APPEARS A MIRROR
A LOOKING GLASS OF OLD
A KEEPER OF TOLLS

THE PRICE TO PAY
MY OWN REFLECTION
MY OWN ACCEPTANCE
MY OWN INCEPTION

RESURRECTION
AFTER
RESURRECTION

I'M FINALLY
FULL BUT IT HURTS

I'M FINALLY
SOBER BUT IT BURNS

I'M FINALLY
HEALED BUT IT TURNS

LIKE MIDNIGHT MOLASSES
STILL UNDIGESTED

[-A PENANCE UNEXPECTED.]

IT'S AN
OVERCROWDED HOUSE
HERE IN MY MOUTH
HERE IN THIS
GLUTTONED GUT
HERE IN THIS
BLOATED BOAT OF
FLESH

THERE ARE
UNFAMILIAR STRANGERS
GORMANDIZERS
GRIND LIKE
ENERGIZER
BUNNIES
GROPING GROTESQUE
GENITALS
AND IT SEEMS
THEY HAVEN'T
BATHED THEMSELVES IN
WEEKS

I AM
TRAPPED INSIDE
WITH THEM
AND I AM
SALIVATING FOR
SOME SPACE
CALL THE CONSTABLE
TELL HIM
TO REMOVE
THESE NEMESES
FROM MY PREMISES
TELL HIM TO
CLEAR THE TABLE

SOMETHING'S
REALLY
WRONG
HERE

BUT THEN

IT'S DAWN

THERE'S

✸S✸U✸N✸S✸P✸E✸C✸K✸S✸ ✸S✸L✸I✸C✸I✸N✸G✸

THROUGH MY TONGUE

AND

THEY'RE

SINGING

IN MY SKULL

DON'T

FEAR

MY

DEAR

WE'RE

NEAR

WE'RE

HERE

AND

YOU'RE

JUST

FINALLY

[-FULL.]

THE BRIGHTEST OF DAYS STILL FEED THE NIGHT
THE
GREAT DELUSIONER
THE
GREAT EXECUTIONER
THE EATER OF LIGHT
MY INSIDIOUS RIDDLER MIND
AN ELECTRIFIED BUTTERFLY
SET ALIGHT INSIDE A TIGHT
TOO-FULL SKULL-WROUGHT CAGE
IT WON'T ESCAPE BEFORE IT'S TOO LATE
THROUGH THE ELASTIC STATIC OF MANIC PANIC
I'M TRYING TO DRIVE HALF-ALIVE
THROUGH ERRATIC TRAFFIC
A LITTLE FRIED
A LITTLE FRANTIC
I FIND
I FEEL
A LITTLE UN-SOMATIC
A LITTLE FRIGHT

BUT SHE'S BACK IN THE PASSENGER SEAT AND
THERE'RE ALL THESE
DELICATE SKELETONS
COVERING MY WINDSHIELD

I USED TO FLY TOO

BACK WHEN I WAS NEW
BACK BEFORE HER COUP
NOW I
HIDE IN MY COCOON

AND TRY LIKE HELL
NOT TO FALL
BACK TO SLEEP

BUT IT'S ALREADY TOMORROW

        AND I'M STILL ON DEATH ROW

                [-I GUESS
                    I JUST THOUGHT
                        SOMEONE SHOULD KNOW.]

IF I COULD STILL MY HEART
BUT FOR A MOMENT
I WOULD ESCAPE THIS TORMENT
AND JOIN THEM IN THE ISLE OF THE LIVING
I WOULD LAUGH ALONGSIDE THEM
AS PIGTAILS FLY HIGH UP ON SWINGSETS
I WOULD ESCAPE INTO SPRINGTIME DREAMSCAPES
AND IN DUE TIME
I WOULD WARM THE WINTER OF MY MIND
I'D WATCH THE SUNSET
I WOULD FORGET WHERE THE STORM WENT
BUT I'M STILL NOT HOME IN MY OWN BONES YET
THIS HEART STILL RUNS TOO FAST AND
I'M STILL TRYING TO FASTEN IT IN
WITH ALL THIS HOPE-ROPE
IT'S JUST A LITTLE TRICKIER THAN I THOUGHT

[-TYING ALL THESE KNOTS.]

I AROSE FROM THE ASHES
A FREE PHOENIX
I DREAMED THIS
THE SICK REMIX
FIXED HEART 2.0
STAR OF A NEW SHOW
SHE'D BE IN THE FRONT ROW
AND I WOULD FINALLY KNOW
I AM LOVED
BUT THAT CHAIR REMAINS EMPTY
SHE WILL NEVER COME BACK TO ME
MY SOUL REMAINS TATTERED AND TORN
NO MATTER
HOW MANY TIMES
IT'S REBORN
THE THEATER'S DE-CONSTRUCTING
I AM ONCE AGAIN COMBUSTING

[-I THINK I MAY HAVE DONE
ALL THIS RESURRECTING
FOR NOTHING.]

GO HOME, YOU'RE DRUNK
I WOULD IF I WERE BUT I'M NOT
ANYMORE
IN FACT I HAVE NOT
TOUCHED A DRINK IN
103 DAYS
I'D JUST SLEEP BUT
I STILL CANNOT SEEM TO ESCAPE
THESE MAUDLIN WEBS THAT
BIND MY MIND IN
103 WAYS

[-MY MIND MAY BE SOBER
BUT MY HEART'S DRUNK ANYWAY.]

I WARMED UP YESTERDAY'S
COFFEE IN THE MICROWAVE
TODAY
I
WANTED IT STALE
JUST LIKE MY SOUL
I GUESS I JUST
NEEDED TO KNOW
I WASN'T ALONE
AND THAT IT'S OK
TO FEEL A LITTLE COLD
A LITTLE OLD
A LITTLE LEFT
OVER

[-SOBER.]

THERE'S AN ADDICT IN THE ATTIC
GATHERING COBWEBS
CHOKED BY THE DUST
OF THIS MONOTONOUS NORMALCY
I DON'T DARE MOVE
NOT EVEN AN INCH
LEST THE HIGH HEAR ME
AND RECLAIM MY RESTLESS HEART
FOREVER WANDERING
IF ONLY IN MY OWN HEAD
AT LEAST I'M NOT DEAD

[-OR AM I?]

I'M AN ETCH-A-SKETCH TODAY

ALL

THIN LINES AND GRAYSPACE

I'M

UNTRACED

[-JUST

TIP

ME

OVER

AND

I'LL

E

RASE.]

STATIC ON A 1950' S TELEVISION SET

UNHINGED VINTAGE OFF-SET VIGNETTE

DAMP SOCKS ON WET PAVEMENT

CIRCLES   UPON

CIRCLES UP ON

CIRCLES

OF

PENCIL LEAD

DEAD

HEAD

[-ANHEDONIA.]

IT'S A RAINY DAY
HERE IN THE INSIDE
WHERE DARK IDEAS HIDE
TANGLED UP IN DAMP STRANDS OF HOPE
THEY MAY BE HALF-CHOKED BY LOVE
BUT THEY'RE STILL CRAWLING UP AND UP
THEY'RE STILL HALF-ALIVE
CLAWING THEIR WAY UP TO MY MIND
WHERE THEY WILL LAY THEIR BLACKENED EGGS
ROTTEN TO THE CORE
THIS BRAIN WILL WATER THEM MORE AND MORE
UNTIL THEY HATCH
BY THEN THEIR WORDS WILL BE NO MATCH
FOR THE CORROSION
NO ANTIDOTE FOR THE POISON
EVEN THE BEST PILLS CANNOT STILL THIS
EVEN THEIR BEST SKILLS WILL NOT KILL THIS

[-THIS MENTAL ILLNESS.]

CHASE ONE
THEY AFTER ANOTHER

LIKE UNWELL CARNIVAL CAROUSEL LOVERS
THEY RUN TILL THEY'VE WORN THEMSELVES DOWN

HORSES BROKE-DOWN GO
HORROR ON A MERRY ROUND

TWISTED HANGING HOPING PARAMOURS
POLES ON FOR TO IN
GRASPED DEAR LIVE A
BY LIFE HOPING TWISTED
TWISTED AS THEY TO UP
SOULS RIDE DIE OBSESSION

[-ANXIETY/DEPRESSION.]

NO ONE TALKS ABOUT THE BOREDOM

THE HUMDRUM
AT THE BORDERS
OF MY MIND
I SUCCUMB
TO THE BORDER-
LINE

JUST TO FEEL SOMETHING

COME BACK UP FROM THE WILDERNESS

I MUST
CONFESS
I PREFERRED
THE MESS
BALLERINAS STAGED
IN A PRETTY CAGE

JUST TO FEEL NOTHING

JUST

GIMME

THAT

DIAGNOSIS

JUST

GIMME

THAT

PSYCHOSIS

I NEED TO FEEL SOMETHING

NO ONE TALKS ABOUT THE WHOREDOM

THE NORMAL
THAT WE'RE PAID
TO FIND
THEY PAY IN HAZY PRAISE
FOR VULNERABILITY AND
EMOTIONAL MATURITY
JUST TALK ABOUT YOUR FEELINGS
OH
BUT IF I TOLD THEM WHAT I'VE FELT
THEY WOULD SURELY MELT
FROM THE UNWELL HELL
THEN GUILT ME FOR THE WELTS

JUST TO BLAME SOMETHING

NO ONE TALKS ABOUT THE STARDOM

THAT COMES WITH BEING CRAZY
THE RUSH FROM
THE RIVERS OF INSANITY
THE PLUSH LEGACY
I WAS GOING TO LEAVE
BEHIND ME
AS I WENT OUT WITH A BANG
LIKE COBAIN
OR VAN GOGH
OR PLATH
I STILL DREAM ABOUT
WHAT IT'D BE LIKE
TO GO OUT LIKE THAT

JUST TO BE SOMETHING

SO THEY CAN TELL ME AGAIN
ABOUT VULNERABILITY AND
EMOTIONAL MATURITY AND
HOW I SHOULD TALK ABOUT MY FEELINGS
TELL ME HOW THEY WANT TO KNOW ME
AND THEN LEAVE ME
ONCE THEY LEARN OF MY FRAGILITY
THEY CAN GO AHEAD AND ANESTHETIZE ME
DE-SENSITIZE AND PARALYZE ME
GENERALIZE AND UN-TRAUMATIZE ME
MAKE ME HEALTHY AND NEW
I'LL STILL BE DRAWN TO A DARKER HUE
BEHIND CLOSED DOORS
I'M REALLY NOT TRYING TO BE UNTOWARD

[-I'M JUST SO FUCKING BORED.]

THE PARTY'S
IN FULL SWING BUT THERE'RE
ARACHNIDS IN THE CUPCAKES
THAT NO ONE ELSE
CAN REALLY SEEM
TO SEE

I SMILE
WITH MY LIPSTICKED MOUTH
BUT MY MIND'S SPLIT ITS STITCHES
AND NO ONE ELSE
CAN REALLY SEE
IT BLEED

THEY'RE CIRCLED IN CROWDS
AS THEY ALWAYS ARE
WITH ALL THEIR PRIDE
AND THEIR HEALED-UP SCARS
AS THOUGH I'M THE ONLY ONE
WHO CAN'T SEEM TO GET OVER
WHAT WAS DONE TO ME

AS THOUGH
I CRAVE THE ABNORMALITY
AS THOUGH
I ACTUALLY WANT
TO BE THIS LONELY
AS THOUGH
I AM NOT SCREAMING SILENTLY
FOR SOMEONE
TO COME
AND SAVE ME

SO THEY CAN HAVE
THEIR CAKE AND EAT IT
I HOPE THEY DON'T MIND MINE
WHEN I FEED IT
TO THE BIRDS
AS I WATCH
THE SPIDERS SCATTER

THE PARTY'S
IN FULL SWING AND THERE'RE
ARACHNIDS IN THE CUPCAKES
BUT YA
IT IS
TOTALLY ME
WHO'S CRAZY

[-T

O

T

A

L

L

Y.]

THE FLOOR OF HELL IS LAIN WITH SHELLS
AND THE FEET OF THE DAMNED ARE DELICATE TELLS
OF ALL THE PLACES WHERE
WE WERE ALL TOO MUCH
OURSELVES
ALL TOO
EXPOSED
ALL TOO
UNWELL
WE FELL
NOT ON OUR OWN
WE WERE FLOWN
DOWN BY WINDS OF CONTEMPT
CONDEMNED
BY THOSE
WHO SWORE
THEY LOVED US

THE EGGS ARE LAID BY THE UNASHAMED
AND THE FATE OF THE DAMNED
IS A DELICATE GAME
TO LEAVE NO TRACES WHERE
WE WERE ALL TOO MUCH
OURSELVES
CAN'T BE
EXPOSED
CAN'T SHOW WE'RE
UNWELL
WE SWELL
WITH MADNESS GROWN
THERE ALL ALONE
UNSOUND WITH SCARS OF
HUMANITY
INSANITY
CLOSED
FROM THEIR
REDEMPTION

[-BUT MENTAL ILLNESS ISN'T A SIN.]

ON A SCALE OF

ONE···TO···TEN

ONE···TO···TEN

CAN I WEIGH MY PAIN

WEIGH IT AGAIN

WITH TEN THE WORST I'VE

EVER FELT

EVER FELT

SCALE __________

CAN I PUT IT A

ON

ON A SCALE UP

I' VE
HEARD THIS ONE
BEFORE
THIS ONE BEFORE
A GIRL WALKS
THROUGH THE DOOR
WALKS THROUGH THE DOOR
BUT I CAN' T TELL IF
IT' S DÉJÀ VU
DÉJÀ VU
I CAN' T TELL IF
WHAT THEY SAY IS TRUE

IT' S NOT TRUE

I COULD'VE SWORN THAT
I'VE JUMPED BEFORE
I'VE JUMPED BEFORE
IN ANOTHER LIFE
ANOTHER LIFE I
SHOULD'VE WORN WHITE
SHOULD'VE WORN WHITE
BUT I WORE RED
I WORE RED

I WORE RED FOR THE EFFECT

I

DIDN'T KNOW DEATH

WAS AN ILLUSION

AN ILLUSION

I'M STILL RETCHING FROM

THE CONFUSION

THE CONFUSION

AND ALL THE MEDS

ALL THE MEDS

ALL THE

MEDS

ALL

THE

ME

D

S

SO LET ME LET YA IN
ON A LITTLE SECRET DOC
I'LL TELL YA THIS ONE
TELL YA OFF THE CLOCK
GO AHEAD AND KEEP IT
IN A LOCKET
KEEP IT REAL SAFE
IN THE POCKET
OF THAT LABCOAT

I'LL SPEAK REAL SLOW
I'LL SPEAK REALLY SLOWLY
KNOW THAT KIDS LIKE ME
KNOW THAT KIDS LIKE ME
WE'RE
ALWAYS AT A TEN
ALWAYS AT A TEN
WE
JUST LEARN TO KEEP IT IN
LEARN TO KEEP IT IN

PAINT ON
A SMILE

PAINT ON
NORMAL

SO WHEN I TELL YOU
I'M ALIVE
WHEN I TELL YOU
THAT I'M FINE
WHEN I LIE
WITH MY BASELINE FIVE
AND IT SOUNDS PLASTIC
IT SOUNDS SARCASTIC
KNOW THAT IT IS
BUT KNOW THAT I'LL LIVE
AND SO WILL THEM

[-W-I--TH
TENS
ETCH----ED
IN-
S-I-D---E
OUR
SK----------IN.]

IT'S STILL DARK HERE
NEAR THE GRIEVING WAVES
I. SANK INTO BLACK SAND
I DRANK IN THE GRAVES OF
LOST LOVES AND STOLEN STRANGERS
//YET I FEEL NO DANGER//
ALTHOUGH. I CAN'T TASTE THE SUN
ALTHOUGH I CANNOT EMBRACE THE MOON
I'M HERE WITH YOU
AND REDWOODS GROW
BURSTING. THROUGH THE OCEAN FLOOR
BURSTING THROUGH MY VERY CORE
AN ANOMALY OF THE SEA

[-NEW FOREST, SAME ME.]

ENVISION ME BY THE SEA
STILL COVERED IN LEAVES
IMAGINE THE BREEZE KNEES
MY
FROM
UP
RISE
I
AS

LOSING MY RELIGION
REBORN IN UNHOLY SALTWATER
I USED TO WISH
SHE'D BRING ME HERE
BACK WHEN I WAS YOUNGER
AND SHE WAS STILL MY GOD

[-BUT NOW I ONLY WORSHIP LOVE.]

HOPE IS
A FLUTTER IN THE LUNG
A STUTTER ON THE TONGUE
A STOP SIGN BEFORE THE CLIFF
THAT LEADS TO THE ABYSS
THE WAIT-A-SECOND BLISS
BEFORE THE COLLECTIVE FALL
[-HOPE IS A REDEMPTIVE WALL.]

BREATHE FOR ME

AND I WILL BREATHE FOR YOU

TAP THE PAGE

TO THE RHYTHM

OF YOUR HEARTBEAT

I WILL HEAR IT

OUR COLLECTIVE ECHO

1···2···1···2···1···2

THESE DEMONS FEED ON

THE FAÇADE OF ISOLATION

ESCAPE YOUR MIND INTO MINE

AND I WILL FIND

MY SOLACE

WITHIN YOURS

PART: THREE.FIVE

[-A COGNITION INTERMISSION.]

ALAS

FRACTURES IN THE GLASS

MY REFLECTION REVEALED A SHATTERED SOUL

BUT I WAS WHOLE ALL ALONG

PART: FOUR

[-THE KEEPING OF SOULS.]

I CAN FEEL THE PULSE OF YOU
FLUTTERING IN THE DARK
LET ME FILL THE HOLES IN YOU
THE HOLES IN YOUR HARD HEART

FOR WHAT IT'S WORTH
I KNOW IT HURTS TO GO
STUMBLING THROUGH THIS SHITSHOW
LIKE WE'RE SUPPOSED TO FEEL GRATEFUL
FOR THIS BROKEN BURNING BALL OF DIRT
WE LIVE ON
WHERE OUR BROKEN BURNING WALLED-UP HURT
LOVED ONES
LIVE ON
BREAKING US
AS THEY BREAK THEMSELVES

AND IT SEEMS LIKE THE HOPE
WE'VE SO LONGED TO HOLD ON TO
IS SWALLOWED UP
IN THE SERENITY
OF SWEET SURRENDER

BUT REMEMBER

WHILE I MAY NOT BE ABLE TO
STEAL THOSE TEARS FROM YOU
REST ASSURED, MY LOVES,
I'LL KEEP ON REMINDING YOU
THAT I CRY WITH YOU

MY HEART PULSES WITH YOU
MY SOUL COURSES WITH YOU
AND YOU WILL NEVER BE ALONE

[-EVEN WHEN I AM NOT WITH YOU,
I AM WITH YOU.]

BORN UNDER INCANDESCENT SNOWGLOBES
WE DON'T FEEL THE GLASS HEATING
BEFORE IT SHATTERS
FOR WE ARE CHILDREN OF THE FIRE
RECONSTRUCTED ON THE PYRE
RESURRECTED FROM THE WOMBS
OF THE COMBUSTING DEMONESSES

AND NOTHING
IS AS
IT ONCE SEEMED

TORN UNDER IGNOBLE KNIGHTS WITH MELTED ARMOR
THEY TOAST WITH LIQUID COURAGE
ATOP HIGH HORSES
FOR WE ARE FAR PAST EVER-AFTER
WHERE THE WICKED STAND ON LADDERS
SPITTING BULLETS FROM THE PULPITS
OF THE SORDID STUMBLING BEAST-PRIESTS

AND NOTHING
IS AS
WE ONCE DREAMED

SHARP SHARDS OF MARVELOUS ILLUSION
TIRED EYES BLINDED BY THE LIGHT
OF OUR OWN LIES
GLITTER DOMES TURN INTO MIRRORBALLS
MOLDING OUR HEARTS INTO FROZEN FEARBALLS
PHANTASMAGORICAL REFLECTIONS
OF A TRANSMOGRIFIED REALITY

[-LET US BREAK FREE.]

AM I ME
OR AM I YOU
I'M NOT SURE ANYMORE

THERE'S A VEIL FROM THE

BOTTOM OF THE OCEAN FLOOR

HEAVENS
THE
TO
UP

AND WE ALL HIDE BEHIND IT
BLUSHING BRIDES
DOUBTING WE DESERVE
TO ADORN OURSELVES IN WHITE

I CAN'T SEE YOU
THROUGH ALL THIS LACE

BUT I CAN FEEL YOU
IN MY VEINS

HOPELESS HARLOTS

TRYING TO HIDE THE SCARLET
BUT IT JUST KEEPS SEEPING THROUGH
YES
IT JUST KEEPS BLEEDING THROUGH

WOUNDS

OF THOSE WHO CAME BEFORE US
AND THOSE WHO WILL COME LONG AFTER WE ARE GONE

BUT WE WERE ONCE ONE

AND I CAN HEAR HEELS CLICKING WHEN I SLUMBER
WALKING THE AISLE TO AN EMPTY ALTAR

RANCID WRAITHS

TRYING TO HIDE THE WEIGHT
BUT THERE'RE LEADEN SNAKES UNDER OUR TRAINS
YES
THOUGHT DRAINS FROM OUR OWN BRAINS

STAINS

OF THOSE WHO CAME BEFORE US
AND THOSE WHO WILL COME LONG AFTER WE ARE GONE

BUT WE REMAIN ONE

ARE YOU ME?
OR ARE YOU YOU?

I'M

NO LONGER

ANYMORE

SURE

THIS SUBCONSCIOUS ILLNESS COMES BETWEEN US

SOMEONE OPEN THE DOOR

SOMEONE RESTORE

OUR COLLECTIVE RAPPORT

OUR ROTTING CORE

[-SEND____A______MENTAL____________METEOR.]

LONELY BUT NEVER ALONE
THE GHOSTS HAVE ALWAYS ROAMED
UNDER MY BED
AND

BALLERINAS TWIRL UP INSIDE MY HEAD

I WAS BORN A LITTLE TOO HOLLOW
I DON'T HAVE THE BONES
TO WRITE THIS POEM
OR MAKE IT TILL TOMORROW

BUT I HEARD YOU'RE HOLLOW TOO
I HEARD YOUR SORROW TOO
I HEARD YOU SCREAMING THROUGH
MOUTHFULS OF BURNING COALS

SO MAYBE WE CAN FILL THESE HOLES TOGETHER
MAYBE WE CAN PAY THESE TOLLS TOGETHER
WE CAN GROW BACK BONES UNALONE

[-THE KEEPING OF SOULS.]

CAN SOMEONE

S TOP. THE

CON

SUMP

TION

SLAVES TO THE MOOD-FOOD WE CONSUME

WE CAN'T FACE IT

WE COVER THE STENCH OF DISPLACEMENT

WITH STOLEN BOTTLES OF DOOM-PERFUME

BUT THAT'S

NOTH

ING

NEW

WE STUFF AND WE STUFF
BUT IT'S NEVER ENOUGH
TO KEEP US FROM FLOATING AWAY
BLOATED WITH SHAME
AND
EIGHT-DOLLAR LATTES
AS OUR HOPE DECOMPOSES
AND
WE START TO DECAY
WE PILE
SADNESS-MAGGOTS
ON OUR BROKEN PLATES

BUT THE MENTALLY ILL STILL SAY GRACE.

BECAUSE WE KNOW THE MADNESS KEEPS US
LACED UP
IT KEEPS US SANE
BECAUSE WE KNOW IT'S INSANE
WE KNOW IT SHOULD SUFFOCATE OUR BRAINS
BEING TRAPPED IN THIS PLACE
IN THESE CONFINES OF BLOOD AND FLESH
AWAITING A PROLONGED DEATH
WHEN OUR HEARTS ARE BLACK HOLES
AND OUR SOULS
ARE UNIVERSES BURSTING WITHIN
UNDERNEATH THIS SLASHED AND SCARRED AND
FAR-
GONE
HARDENED
SKIN

BUT

MY LOVES,

ONE DAY THE MADNESS WILL DISPEL

THE STARDUST INSIDE US IS ETHEREAL

AND OUR LOVELUST IS EVER ETERNAL

JUST WAIT

JUST STAY

[-IT'S NOT TOO LATE.]

SOME HEARTS ARE BORN DARK

TAR S L I P P I N G THROUGH CALLOUSED FINGERS

JUST TRYING TO STICK TO SOMETHING TO

AN-
Y
THING

BEFORE THEY HARDEN. BEFORE THEY'RE WALKED ON.

SOME ARE PINK AS A DREAM
UNTIL THEY'RE P-I-E-R-C-E-D→
BY SOMEONE ELSE'S QUILL

UNTIL THE INK SPILLS. UNTIL THE PAIN STAINS.

AND THEY'RE FOREVER CHANGED.

SO

~~~~~~~~~~~~~~~~~~~~~~~~~~~~~~~~

I WILL SWIM THROUGH RIVERS OF BLACK BLOOD

WITH YOU

I WILL BATHE IN OCEANS OF OBSIDIAN MUD

~~~~~~~~~~~~~~~~~~~~~~~~~~~~~~~~

I NEVER NEEDED OUR LOVE TO BE
BLEACHED WHITE ANYWAY
I'M A LITTLE TOO TIRED OF THE SNOW ANYWAY

OUR HEARTS CAN JUST MELT INTO ONE
UNDER THE HEAT OF THIS BOILING SUN

WE WILL SURVIVE AS

S T AR D US T

DOES
MY LOVES

WE WILL STIR UP LIFE

AS LOVELUST DOES

[-DON'T FORGET WE WERE ONE ONCE.]

I AM THE LIGHT AND THE DARK
RAINBOW-TINTED BLOOD MARKS
STREAKED ACROSS THE MOON

I SUMMON IT FROM THE SKY
I SWALLOW IT EVERY NIGHT

I DROWN IN THE FRENZY
OF UNRIGHTEOUSNESS
MEET ME IN THE DEPTHS
OF OUR UNCONSCIOUSNESS

IT MAY BE MESSY
BUT IT IS FREE
AND WHAT IS EMPATHY
IF NOT THE ABILITY
TO GO
DOWN
DOWN
DOWN
INTO
ANOTHER

COME DROWN WITH ME
IN SEAS OF SYMBIOTIC SYNERGY
THE DARK PARTS
WILL LIGHT OUR WAY
INTO ENLIGHTENED UNITY

YOU ARE THE LIGHT AND THE DARK
RAINBOW-TINTED BLOOD MARKS
STREAKED ACROSS THE MOON

YOU SUMMON IT FROM THE SKY
YOU SWALLOW IT EVERY NIGHT

[-YOU & I.]

I' VE BEEN PICTURING IT LATELY
AT THE EDGE OF THE SEA
OF MY DREAMS
WHEN ALL HAS BEEN RENDERED USELESS
EXCEPT FOR THIS EFFORTLESS TRANSCENDENT LOVE

I SEE YOU THERE

WHEN OUR BROKEN BODIES REACH
THE EXTENT OF THEIR TOIL
AFTER ALL
AND OUR LIMITLESS HEARTS HAVE
MET THEIR LIMITATIONS FOR INJUSTICES

I SEE YOU THERE

YOUR OMNIPRESENCE EMANATES
WHERE IT DIDN'T BEFORE
YOU'RE WITH ME
MY PENANCE IN BROKEN REMNANTS
WHEN I WILL ARRIVE AT YOUR DOOR IN THE END

I SEE YOU THERE

I'LL FEEL YOUR HEART PULSING IN THE STARS
WELL AFTER THE WORLD GOES DARK
OUR LOVE STAYS
I'VE BEEN ENVISIONING IT LATELY
I'VE BEEN WISHING IT WITHOUT MY OWN CONSENT

I SEE YOU THERE

I DON'T PAINT PRETTY PICTURES
NOR PEN FAIRY TALES
TELL ME NOW
WHAT HAPPENS IN THAT FINAL HOUR
IN THE LAST PAGES OF YOUR EVER-AFTERS

[-AM I THERE?]

I HAVE BEEN PREPARING FOR THIS VERY MOMENT

LOOK AROUND

HERE WITH YOU
HERE RIGHT NOW

YOU SING IN SILENT SYMPHONY
AND THE OCEAN HAS BEEN EMPTIED
BY THE SOUND

YOUR LOVE IS LOUD
IT DROWNS OUT
THE WICKED WAVES
IT BREAKS THE SICKENED CLOUDS
INSIDE MY MOUTH

I STAND UPON BLACK SAND
WITH YOUR HAND IN MY HAND
AND LAUGH AT THE PAST
AS ANOTHER SPELL IS CAST
AND WE ARE BOUND

LOOK AROUND

HERE WITH YOU
HERE RIGHT NOW

ELEPHANTS ARE
RISING FROM THE GROUND
A STAMPEDE OF RESONANCE
IMPRINTS PERMANANCE
SHROUDS THE DOUBT

SWIRLS THROUGH WORLDS

THROUGHOUT LIFETIMES
UPON LIFETIMES
UPON LIFETIMES

[-OUR LOVE
GOES
ROUND
AND
ROUND.]

WHO NEEDS A HEAVEN?
WHO NEEDS ATONEMENT?
I'M ALREADY LIVING ETERNITIES
WITH YOU IN THIS MOMENT.

Milton Keynes UK
Ingram Content Group UK Ltd.
UKHW020913281123
433369UK00002B/11/J

9 780228 875192